Z's
REFLECTIONS

Also by Ann Zwemer:

Professional Adjustments and Ethics for Nurses in India
seven editions

Basic Psychology for Nurses in India
two editions

Just a Moment
two editions

Longings

Z's

REFLECTIONS

Poems & Thoughts For Seasons, Holidays and More

Ann Zwemer

WESTBOW
PRESS®
A DIVISION OF THOMAS NELSON
& ZONDERVAN

WestBow Press books may be ordered through booksellers or by contacting:

WestBow Press
A Division of Thomas Nelson & Zondervan
1663 Liberty Drive
Bloomington, IN 47403
www.westbowpress.com
1 (866) 928-1240

ISBN: 978-1-5127-0180-7 (sc)
ISBN: 978-1-5127-0181-4 (e)

Library of Congress Control Number: 2015919938

Print information available on the last page.

WestBow Press rev. date: 02/19/2016

And It Is You
(A prayer of dedication)

As a child,
my life
began:
shy, speechless,
feeling deeply.
There seemed to be
a pair of me.
It was I, Lord,
and it was You.

As an adult,
I stand before you,
no longer shy
or speechless
because
there is
a pair of me.
It is I, Lord,
and it is You.

Ann Zwemer 2008

As a teen,
I dreamed of
changing the world
and in my shyness
believed
there was
a pair of me.
It was I, Lord,
and it was You.

As a woman over eighty,
I often wonder
what lies ahead,
always believing
everything will be okay
because there is
a pair of me,
It is I, Lord,
and it is You.

Ann Zwemer 2013

Foreword

Words.

I'm Dr. Jim Brown: husband, father, son, brother, community leader, educator, author, professor, friend, and pastor. It is in these last two roles that I know Ann Zwemer, the "Z" in *Z's Reflections*. I lead The Lake Church (a.k.a. The United Church of Lake San Marcos) and teach graduate educational technology and psychology courses for Azusa Pacific University. I've known Ann for over a year as her pastor and friend and know her to be a resoundingly unusual woman. She has listened to me speak and teach weekly and has been a cheerleader and encourager, and we have worked together in our community to help those who are in need of encouragement, enlightenment, and hope. We provide those uplifting qualities by our words.

Words.

Words are a *key* difference between humans and the rest of the animal kingdom.

Ann, a former nurse and, with her late doctor husband, missionary to India, is a gifted thinker and writer. She has written much prior to this book: textbooks on nursing, books to inspire. Ann wrestles with words and reaches deep inside herself to find just the right combination of words that will make a difference in the reader.

You have in your hands a book of many well-chosen words.

Ann's life has been one of *service* and *care* for others. As a nurse, she was taught—and then taught other nurses—to assess the situation and then bring whatever care options made the most sense and contributed the most healing to the patient, never losing sight of the fact that this "patient" was, first and foremost, a person, a human being made in the image of God. Therefore, he or she deserved the *best* that that nurse could offer.

Ann has brought her *best* to this book.

This book can last you a year. If you take the year and read and consume it slowly, you'll discover a year's worth of uplifting inspiration. You'll find a neutralizer for at least some of the "news" you digest regularly. You'll also develop the *habit* of reading good words.

This book matters.

Why does this book matter? Because it is written *for you*. You hold in your hands a book of well-chosen words and thoughts that can *help you* be a better you: a better husband, wife, daughter, son, worker, boss, Christian.

The books you read.

You've started the journey by picking up this book. Now I encourage you to delve into Ann's writings, into this book, and let the positive *words* touch, inspire, and lift you up.

Blessings,

Dr. Jim Brown

Preface

It is a unique privilege to gather a lifetime of writing and share it with you. Because I spent so many years writing textbooks for nurses in India, most of these writings were done during the last decade.

My style of writing has developed from preparing textbooks for students learning in a second language and from my becoming legally blind. These two elements created in me a need to express meaningful thought in as few words as possible in an easy-to-read format.

The preparation of *Z's Reflections* was immeasurably assisted by my very good friend, Llona Kitzing (LaNay), who played various important roles in getting the book published. Beginning with a vibrant vision of the end result, she helped to organize it as a calendar, closely editing and proofing each piece and always thinking creatively with me. I am also very grateful to my sister, Betty Zuverink, who patiently read my material and helped me to format my lines creatively in the book. Finally, I thank Doug Saito for his technical assistance in the process of electronically publishing this book.

Ann Zwemer

Contents

The First

Beginning
the New Year
is like standing
on the seashore
at first light,
looking out at
the vast expanse
of divinely brushed,
smooth-as-silk sand
after the tide
has come and gone,
not leaving
a single footprint
of yesterday,
waiting for me
to make
the first.

The Parade of Time

Time
is a mystery
fashioned by the
hands of God,
a parade
without end.
Its colorful
seasonal banners
march by, one at a time,
fluttering vigorously
in the winds of
cold and warmth,
rain and shine.
It steps reluctantly
to the beat of
life's drums,
a rhythm
created by
sunrise and sunset,
old and new,
sadness and joy.
It comes at last
full circle
as it embraces
the new year
and goes on...
and on...
and on....

Ann Zwemer

It Is Good

I live my life
in cycles,
each of which
is good,
cherished
for its unique
characteristics,
explaining why,
when I am
once again
alone,
I can say,
"This, too,
is good."

Z-1

It is good
to wake up
and think,
"I love
who I am!"

Z-2

I will always
be happy
if
I aim
to make
God happy.

Z-3

I should
never
question
what
God
can do.

Z-4

Contentment
is
a natural
goal
in life.

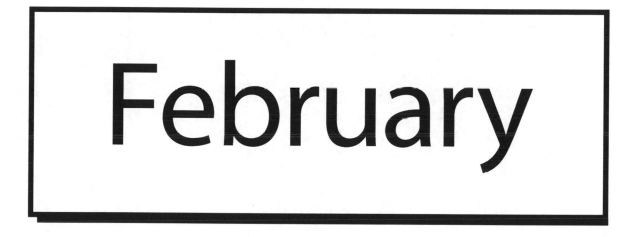

Ann Zwemer

Happy Valentine's Day

I'm so glad

my

journey

through life

included

you.

My Heart

I look
with envy
at the
inscribed candies,
rich chocolates,
and pretty cards
with
arrow-pierced hearts,
red flowers,
secret notes—
all for others,
wishing
they were for me
until
I realize
Valentine's Day
is the day
I, too,
could give
my heart away.

Longings

The deepest
longing
of my soul
is
to be
made whole.

The deepest
longing
of my heart
is
to be
loved.

The deepest
longing
of my aloneness
is
to be
touched.

Mis-Understanding

I cannot describe
how despair
ravages my soul
when I believe
a dear one is
no longer there
just because
we differ in thought:
nor can I describe
how peace swathes
this same soul
when we are
once again
united.

Z-5

Technology
has become
the
new world
to all
humankind.

Z-6

I feel
good
when
I follow
the direction
of my heart.

Z-7

If I come
to God
regularly,
I will often
be able
to find God.

Z-8

Hearing
just
happens
while
listening
pays attention.

March

Ann Zwemer

Spring!

It's not
a world
I can make.
It's not
a world
you can make.
It's
all new!
It's
all fresh!
It's
all clean!
It's
all green!
It's
God's world!
It's
spring!

The Gap

I strive
to close
the
gap
I first meet
in separation
from
my mother,

for I feel
there is
a gap
between my soul
and my humanness
a gap
too wide
for me to close

then find
the gap
between me,
and others
which all of
my striving
leaves
untouched,

until
I find God
who
reaches out
and draws me in
to close
the gap
for all eternity.

A Reason for Being

When I am young,
my world
is filled with
reasons for
being!
One by one,
they fade
from
my consciousness
until
I wonder,
Why am I here?
Even then
I know
there is *always*
a reason
that I must
identify
and embrace,
a reason
for
my being.

Z-9

Where
there is
sound,
there is
life.

Z-10

I will
hear
God
only if
I am still.

Z-11

Computers
can be
just as
unpredictable
as people.

Z-12

*Be still
and know
that
I am
God.*

Psalms 46:10 NIV

April

My Jesus Walk

It is Lent.
Striving
to live
more like
Jesus,
I give up sweets for six weeks,
identifying with Christ's sacrifice
at Calvary,
believing
God's
love and
mercy
will accept
even this
pitiful,
imperfect
sacrifice
from me
as part
of my
Jesus walk.

Easter

Easter
is celebrated
as a symbol of
hope.
To me, it means
life after
death,
gladness after
sadness,
success after
failure,
healing after
pain,
joy after
tears,
peace after
conflict—
all of this
because
Jesus Christ
rose from
the dead.

Ann Zwemer

Lost and Found

When I lost
my eyesight,
I fell into
the blues,
craving to bring
my eyesight back,
keep it from
escaping again.
Then
I lost the blues
because
I found,
as my eyesight
became less,
my soul sight
became more.

Z-13

"Why?"
is a
question
often
left
unanswered.

Z-14

My culture
dictates
much
of my
ethics.

Z-15

If I meet
my spiritual needs
first,
all other needs
will eventually
be met.

Z-16

Fads
are fun
but temporary,
not deserving
a permanent
place
in my life.

May

Ann Zwemer

A Birthday Clock

My birthday
starts a clock
ticking
as it records
the days
of my life:
ticking through
early days,
innocent,
childlike
abandon;
ticking through
adolescent days,
rushing toward
freedom and
independence;
adult days,
challenges and
self-fulfillment;
it stops ticking
only
when I pass
through
the thin veil
separating me
from God's
eternity.

Music

Music plays
the keyboard
of my soul.
Sometimes
I need a colon
or a semicolon;
sometimes
a full stop,
a period.
Even then
I can hear
music continue
to echo
off the walls
of my heart
as it feeds
my soul.

Ann Zwemer

A Memorial Day Experience

I go to the cemetery on
Memorial Day.

I stand
wrapped
in the stillness
of death.
It is easy
to feel,
"God is here."

I think
about the
soldiers and
my loved ones.
I wonder,
"Did they feel
God was here?"

I return
to the
cacophony
of everyday life.
To my delight,
I feel
"God is even here!"

Z-17

When
things
are good,
I cling
to the
"now."

Z-18

Loss
is a
reality
of
life.

Z-19

Clothing
without
pockets
is hardly
worth
buying.

Z-20

I should
learn
to adjust
to whatever
I cannot
change.

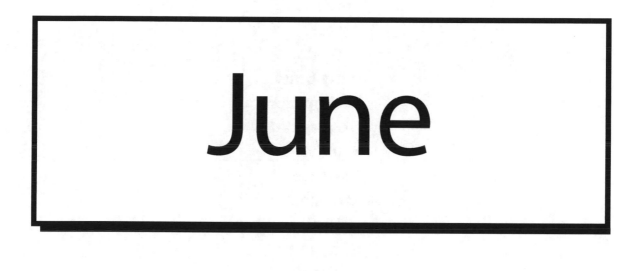

June

Ann Zwemer

Summertime Rest

Summer
means
vacation.
Vacation
means
rest.
Rest
for my body
is simple
to plan:
fun activities,
exercise,
extra sleep.
Rest
for my mind
is simple
to plan, too:
shut down
phones, mail,
computers,
keyboards.
Rest
for my spirit
then comes
unplanned,
copiously
bathing
my soul.

The Graduate

The graduate
is
a person
set apart
for a moment
to celebrate
a personal achievement
that cannot be seen
but is of great value
for a lifetime.
Be proud!
Be excited!
Be delighted!
Be celebrated!

God Awareness
(Touching Base with God)

God awareness
is something I want.
My awareness of God,
knowing God is present,
influences what I believe,
how I relate to others,
how I relate to God.

I need to program
God awareness
into my personal life.
It may be a prayer,
many regular prayers,
Christian meditation,
Scripture-reading,
sacred music.
Whatever helps me
touch base with God
gives me God awareness.

Z-21

Exercise
is the key
to health
of body,
mind,
and spirit.

Z-22

*I can do
everything
through Christ
who gives me
strength.*

—Philippians 4:13 NIV

Z-23

To have
no regrets
is
a healthy
goal.

Z-24

The first
of anything good
is
usually
the best.

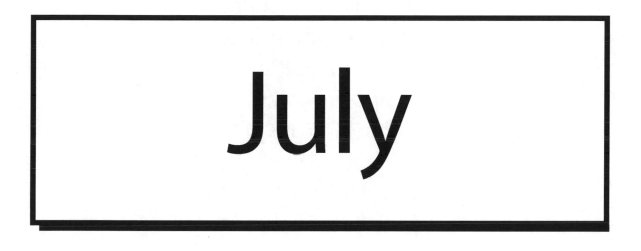

July

Ann Zwemer

I Am Free!

I can walk
Main Street
of any town
anywhere in my country
on the Fourth of July
with parades
and fireworks,
knowing this is
a land of liberty.
I am free!
I am free
because I accept
the limitations
of freedom.
I am free to speak,
I am free to choose,
I am free to believe,
as long as I practice
the Golden Rule:
"love my neighbor as myself."

Bound

I want
to be free,
yet
feelings
bind me
like leather straps
drawn so tightly
they take
my breath away
until
I learn
to master the
controls.

Ann Zwemer

A Unique People of God
(For a Church Anniversary)

We are the- - - - -Church of
- -
a unique people of God,
an integral part
of the outside world,
celebrating our
____th Anniversary.

We look back upon
____years of time,
a long time
to us,
a fleeting moment
to God!

We look back upon
____years
of change.
Pastors come and go,
Board presidents,
Committees, come and go—
a changing people
in a changing world.

We look back upon
____years
of faith:
serving an
unchanging God
through an
unchanging Savior,
our firm
foundation.

We look forward
to unknown years
of time, change,
and faith
here in our community
as we continue to be

a unique people of God.

Z-25

My family tree
tells me who I am
in the eyes
of the world.
The Bible
tells me who I am
in the eyes of God.

Z-26

Life is like
a carousel:
people get on,
people get off,
some people
go in circles!

Z-27

As long as
I can walk,
I feel
a sense
of freedom.

Z-28

It is
a gift
to know
when
to speak.

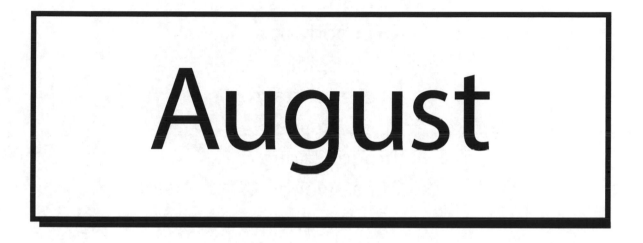

Ann Zwemer

The Mountaintop

When
I have been
on the
mountaintop
in body or
in spirit,
I cannot stay,
so I relive
through thought
those wonders
again and
again and
again.

Alone

When
everything
is over,
everyone
has gone,
I savor
the silence
in which
I finally come
face to face
with myself,
myself
alone.

25 Things I Could Do When I'm Feeling Down

1. Avoid all media news.
2. Call long-distance friends.
3. Write a letter or write in my journal.
4. Talk with somebody—anybody.
5. Encourage an impromptu visitor.
6. Cook or bake a complicated recipe.
7. Sort clothing.
8. Make something for somebody else.
9. Give a gift to somebody.
10. Sort books.
11. Join a support group.
12. Find a new volunteer job.
13. See a good movie.
14. Do a "makeover" of something.
15. Read something uplifting.
16. Play a musical instrument.
17. Set out to do something big and special.
18. Join a Bible study or prayer group.
19. Listen to my favorite music.
20. Eat or drink something I love.
21. Visit, telephone, or e-mail the homebound.
22. Travel.
23. Pray.
24. Meditate.
25. Do what I do best.

Z-29

God
never
takes
a
vacation!

Z-30

Obedience
may
come
before
understanding.

Ann Zwemer

Z-31

I plan
for the
future:
I live
in the
now.

Z-32

Self-approval
dispels
my fear
of
disapproval.

Ann Zwemer

Gentle Fall

When fall
arrives,
it seems
a pause
in the flow
of seasons.
Leaves change,
and begin to drop,
and crops mature
for harvest;
oppressive heat
of summer
is gone,
and cold chill
of winter
is yet to come.
Slanting golden rays
of sunshine
embrace me,
encourage me
to stop,
take a deep
breath,
allow myself
to be wrapped
quietly, gently,
in the warmth
of God's love
as I prepare for
the busy days ahead.

A Labor of Love

I celebrate
Labor Day,
recognizing
the value
of work,
a natural
part of life.

Sometimes
I earn money
by working.

Sometimes
I get sweaty
and dirty
when I work.

Sometimes
I help others
accomplish
a good thing,
feeling great
satisfaction.

Sometimes
I work just
to fill
my own
emptiness.

Whatever
the reason,
my work is
always
a labor of love.

A Divine Plan

I believe
there is
a divine plan
for
my life,
which,
if I find
and
follow,
will produce
only
good
for me
and good
for others.

Z-33

My personal
agenda
is more
powerful
for me
than that of
the group.

Z-34

The same pain
I ignore
while working
keeps me
awake
at night.

Z-35

Everything
has a
beginning.
Everything
has an
end.

Z-36

I can
never
please
everybody!

Z-37

Work
is satisfying.
Play
is refreshing.
I need
both.

Z-38

I can sleep
most
anywhere
if I have
a good
pillow.

Ann Zwemer

My Halloween Mask

When I see
the black mask
of Halloween,
I seldom remember
All Saints Eve,
October 31st
because
I wear a mask
every day.

I don
my mask
whenever I leave
my personal space
to face
the world outside.
My mask
protects
my inner being
from others
as it protects others
from anything
undesirable
in me.

The only time
I am without
my mask
is when I am
alone
or
with God
in prayer.

Beyond Words

As I journey
through life,
I love
others;
others
love me.

I finally
come to
life's
evening hours
when quietness
reigns,
expectations dim.

You come
into
my space,
my heart,
a big surprise
so different
from
any other.

You are
a belated
life gift
to me,
the value
of which
is
beyond words.

Ann Zwemer

Waiting

Waiting …
inevitable,
unavoidable,
most
frustrating,
until
I perceive it …
accept it …
use it …,
an unexpected
gift of time.

Z-39

Technology
changes
so fast
and ethics
struggle
to keep up.

Z-40

I need
to accept
others
who succeed
in my area
of expertise.

Z-41

If I want
to relate,
I
must
communicate.

Z-42

I wish
I could
always
practice what
I preach.

Ann Zwemer

I Give Thanks, Lord

I give thanks, Lord,
because
You are there;
You lift
my spirit.
In Jesus' name,
I give thanks, Lord.

I give thanks, Lord,
even when
my body
is hurting
and my health
is failing.
I give thanks, Lord,
even when
my eyesight
is fading
and my hearing
is gone.
I give thanks, Lord,
even when
I am
losing my
loved ones.
Even then,
Lord,
I give thanks.

I give thanks, Lord,
because
You are there;
You lift up
my spirit.
In Jesus' name,
I give thanks, Lord.

Afterthoughts

Some thoughts
come
naturally
when an event
is over
and everyone
has gone—
thoughts
so important
I need
to tell you
right now.
These are my
afterthoughts.

Ann Zwemer

Leftovers

They were at my door again.
Time to collect food for the needy.
Hmmm, what shall I give?
Ah, yes; spinach, yams, a bean
concoction.
Nobody at home liked these anyway.
Leftovers.

The phone rang often—
Organizations calling for used clothing.
No problem there.
Worn-out shirts and buttonless blouses—
Good to get rid of these things.
Leftovers.

The church was at it again: money.
Urgent pleas for mission!
Don't they know the new principle?
Our own needs come first.
Maybe—at the end of the year.
Leftovers.

Shut-ins were on my prayer list.
Should really go to visit them.
Just must have time for myself.
Everywhere, needs for service, but ….
Surely, someday I'll have some time.
Leftover.

Then suddenly it frightens me.
My giving has gone all wrong!
God gave His Son, His very best.
I saved my best for me.
What if—what if God gave only
leftovers?

Z-43

Older age
excuses me
from
many
things.

Z-44

It may be
easier
to make
a promise
than to keep
a promise.

Z-45

I need
extra energy
to make
a successful
transition.

Z-46

If I plan well
for a transition,
I can make it
a positive
experience.

Two Faces of Winter

Winter
is a season of
contrast:
angry, threatening skies
versus
crystal-clear moonlight;
ice-cold winds
versus
warm, glowing fires;
long, dark nights
versus
cozy, inviting homes;
life-stopping blizzards
versus
snowballs and snowmen;
shivering, numbing chills
versus
bone-warming hot drinks;
stressful study and work
versus
happy family gatherings;
end of the year
versus
beginning of the year;
wondering if God cares
versus
believing God loves us.

Christmas Comes

Year after year
Christmas comes
with
laughter, song,
exuberance, joy.

Year after year
Christmas comes
with
love of dear ones
far and near.

Year after year
Christmas comes
with
a message for all:
"Christ is here!"

Year after year
this Holy Day comes
and brings with it
a Christmas tear.

Z-47

I often
look
at something
without
seeing it.

Z-48

However
I am,
wherever
I am,
I belong
to God.

Z-49

As age
slows me
down,
time
seems to
go faster.

Z-50

It is
always
too late
to
procrastinate.

Ann Zwemer

One More Year

Annual
remembrances
come
again and again
as my
anniversaries,
sad and glad.

My sad
anniversaries
recall
unhappy events,
evoke feelings
of loss, regret,
grief, and heartache,
even bringing tears.

My glad
anniversaries
come more often.
Then I re-live,
re-create
the glad event
with feelings of
happiness,
joy, laughter,
and nostalgic
gratitude,
always ending
with a prayer
asking God
for at least
one more year.

Printed in the United States
By Bookmasters